Make Your Own Art

Collage

FRANKLIN WATTS
LONDON • SYDNEY

First published in 2008 by Franklin Watts

© 2008 Arcturus Publishing Limited

Franklin Watts
338 Euston Road
London NW1 3BH

Franklin Watts Australia
Level 17/207 Kent Street, Sydney, NSW 2000

Produced by Arcturus Publishing Limited,
26/27 Bickels Yard, 151–153 Bermondsey Street,
London SE1 3HA

Editor: Alex Woolf
Designers: Sally Henry and Trevor Cook
Consultant: Daisy Fearns

Picture credits: Sally Henry and Trevor Cook

A CIP catalogue record for this book is available
from the British Library.

Dewey Decimal Classification Number: 702.81'2

ISBN 978 0 7496 8189 0

Printed in China

Franklin Watts is a division of Hachette Children's Books,
an Hachette Livre UK company
www.hachettelivre.co.uk

Contents

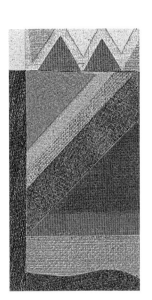

Introduction

'Collage' comes from the French word for glue. It's all about sticking different things together to make pictures. Follow the instructions with your own choice of materials to make a unique artwork.

Collecting materials

You can make your collage out of almost anything. Start off with what you might find in and around your home. Look out for colour, texture and pattern. Always make sure that whatever it is you want to use, you ask first!

Here's a very short list of things to collect.

- **coloured and printed paper**
  – newspapers, magazines, wrapping paper, junk mail, postcards, old tickets
- **fabric** – dressmaking material scraps, knitting wool
- **plastics** – plastic bags, drinking straws, containers and lids, packaging
- **natural things** – dried leaves, twigs, seeds, flowers, tree bark, grasses, feathers
- **dried foods** – peas and beans, grains, pasta shapes
- **things from the seashore** – driftwood, shells, small pebbles

When you find some interesting things together in one place, you may also find that they work well together in a collage.

Shaping your work

Cut neatly round your work with scissors. You can cut close to the edge or leave a border.

Tear paper or card to give a softer edge. This needs practice. Be patient and experiment! If you're tearing strips, you may find that your paper tears best in one direction. Tear paper into small pieces for a torn-paper collage (see page 27).

You can make very straight tears by folding and creasing the paper first. Make a tear by pulling the paper apart, holding it away from the tear line. Change your grip as you go, so that you only have to pull at the point where the paper is tearing.

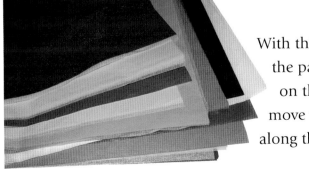

With thinner, lighter papers, it's easier to do this with the paper laying on a surface. Put your hands flat on the paper on each side of the crease and gently move them apart. The paper should tear neatly along the crease.

Background

Try your picture on different backgrounds before you stick it down. Your background could be coloured paper or card, board or even paper plates! Box lids make excellent backgrounds for three-dimensional collage pictures. Try different shapes (see page 18).

Glue

It's important to have the right kind of glue for the material.

- **Glue sticks** are good for sticking paper and thin card together. Put your pieces face down on some clean scrap paper and apply glue evenly on the back. Work from the middle and spread the glue right off the edge and onto the scrap paper. Carefully put the piece in position on your artwork and press down. There should be no surplus glue, blobs or mess.

- **White craft glue** sticks thicker card, heavier fabrics and even wood. It dries clear but takes time to set. Stick flat things with a thin coat of glue on each surface. Press together and set aside to dry. You can stick small but heavy things such as pasta shells to the background by pushing them into a blob of white craft glue. Be very careful when using it with paper. It contains water which may make the paper wrinkle.

Glue

- **Universal glue** comes in a tube and is clear and rubbery. It's good for unusual combinations of materials. Try it with scrap before you use it on your best artwork. It tends to 'string', and this can easily spoil your work.

Display

Try this method for putting your work on display. Take two pieces of card, each 50 x 20mm (2 x 0.75in). Score across the middle of each piece and bend up a little. Use a hole punch to make holes in one end of each piece. Glue them on the back of your background board and attach string between the holes. Now you just need a hook in the wall to hang it from.

Planning

You can start with a drawing or a photograph, or you can just put things together and see what suggests itself. Try and think about the order that you'll need to do things in to get the result that you want. Remember, you're making something to keep.

The office car

This project is all about looking at things in a new way. Most homes have a collection of office bits and pieces somewhere. We've made ours into a car! What can you find? Don't forget to ask if you can have things!

You will need:

- Coloured paper, scissors
- Cardboard, silver paper
- Paper clips, an old CD
- Universal glue
- Any small stationery items, such as: clips, lids, tags, paper fasteners, picture hooks, staples, split rings

15 MINUTES

What to do...

Use coloured paper for the background. We've listed all the bits we started with, but yours can be as different as you like. Sort out your collection and decide which things look like part of a car. Use universal glue to hold heavier things firmly. It will dry clear.

2 MINUTES

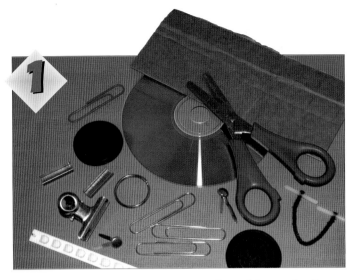

Make sure no-one wants the the old CD before you stick it down! We only need half showing, so cover the rest with the cardboard car shape.

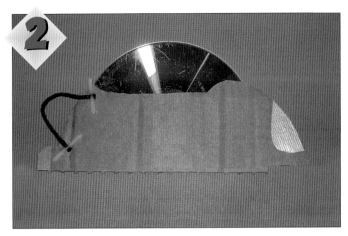

A patch of silver paper goes behind the headlight. The treasury tag makes a good luggage strap.

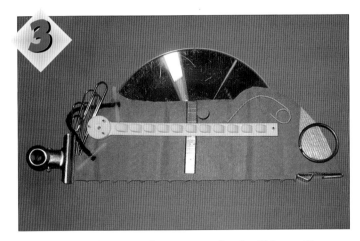

The paper clips are luggage. The bulldog clip becomes a tow-bar. Put a tack on the door for a handle. Stick the plastic picture hook bar on the side panels and put the brass picture hook at the front, for a bumper.

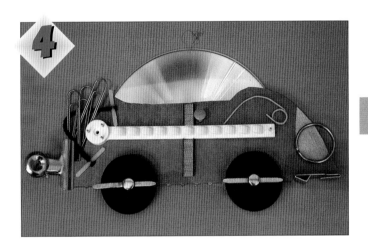

9

The split ring is the headlamp. Wheels are plastic lids with paper fasteners opened and stuck down. We added a pink paper clip for an aerial.
The office car is on the road!

Hints and tips

- Start with something striking. These pieces of hardware have already done half the work of making a funny picture!

Textures

35 MINUTES

5 MINUTES

You will need:

- White paper, thin card, scissors, glue stick
- Pencil, marker pen, paints, brush, tissues
- Old magazines, coloured felt (optional)

What to do...

To create a collage like this you need to make a collection of painted or printed textures. You could even use felt or other fabrics.

Paint textures or cut out pieces of magazines.

Do a simple line drawing on card as a guide.

Cut out the shapes, stick them to the background.

Add figures or animals to complete your picture.

Fun gardening

Whatever the weather, you can make a lovely garden for yourself, indoors.

You will need:

- Coloured card for background
- Different kinds of leaves
- Seed heads or grasses
- Flower buds, twigs
- Scissors, universal glue
- Marker pen
- Wax crayons

40 MINUTES

What to do...

Collect basic materials from your garden or local park. You can use dried seed heads, grasses and flowers. Even if your fresh leaves go brown, your collage will still be an attractive miniature garden!

5 MINUTES

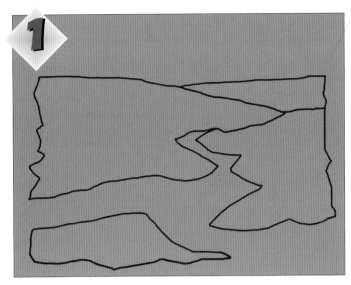

Draw simple outlines for your garden as a guide to building your collage.

Arrange similar objects together to fill areas with interesting patterns and colours.

Fill in open areas with contrasting foliage. Stick each piece down carefully and allow to dry.

Use distinctive elements for trees. Leaves can make bird shapes.

13

Hints and tips

- To add variety to your garden, you can use dried or pressed flowers.
- Use feathers, small shells or stones.
- The landscape on the right is done in crayons. We put in some sprigs of herbs to add interest. We think they look just like trees.

Recycled robot

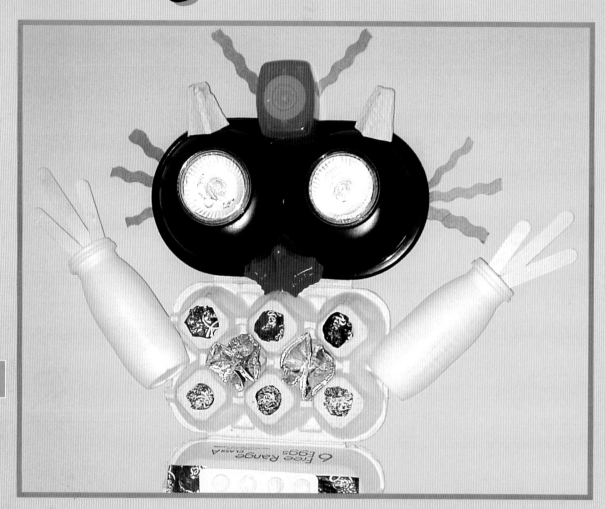

15 MINUTES

2 MINUTES

Bring a pile of bits to life! Robots are all different. Make yours now!

You will need:

- Coloured card for background
- Universal glue
- Assortment of packaging
- Tin foil containers
- Plastic trays and lids
- Sweet wrappers
- Scissors

What to do...

Look out for old packaging and worn out bits and pieces which could become your robot! Ask an adult for things you can use. We found lots of the things in the recycling bin ideal for this project. Sort out what you have been given. Look for round things which could be eyes. Look for stringy things which could be weird hair. Arrange the bits on your background.

1 Check which bits you like. Ignore anything too big and think about what will fit on your card.

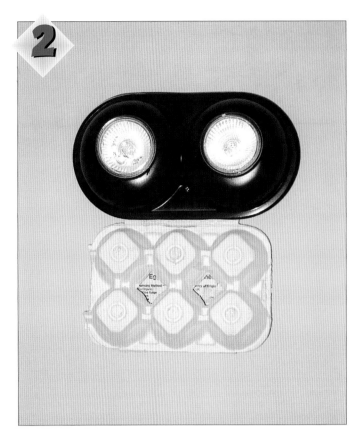

2 We used a plastic vegetable tray and two lids for our robot's head. His body is an egg box.

3 His nose is a red plastic cake tray and his ears are made of bits of egg box.

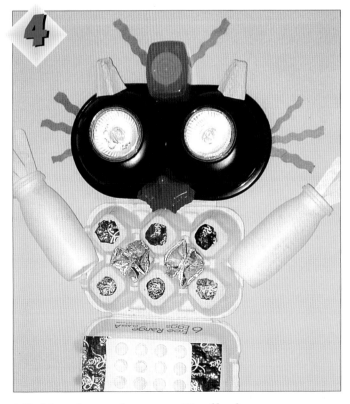

4 Mini bottles make arms. Finally, he gets wavy-cut cardboard hair and an orange head beacon!

Pasta cottage

You will need:

- Pasta shapes, spaghetti
- Scissors, white craft glue
- Poster paints and brushes
- Marker pens, tissues
- Background card

25 MINUTES

What to do...

Check the sizes of your pasta before you start painting. Make sure your house will be big enough for lots of pasta shapes.

5 MINUTES

Paint a simple house, with a roof, walls, chimneys, windows and a door.
Paint the sky blue and the grass green.

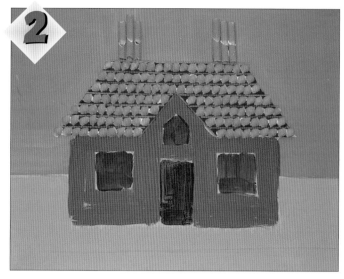

Choose some pasta shell shapes and glue them in rows along the roof. Find some pasta tubes for the chimneys.

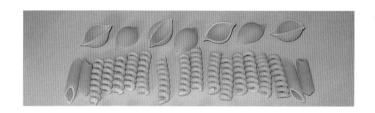

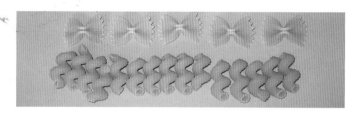

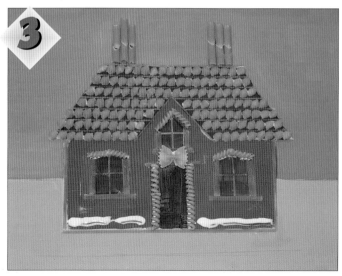

Spiral pasta looks great over the windows and at the sides of the door. Put on more glue and find some bow-tie pasta to decorate the base.

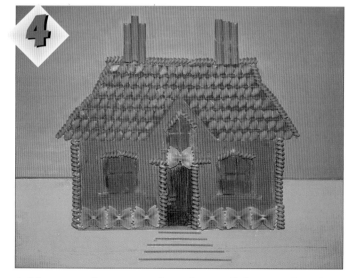

Add more shapes to the edges of the roof and walls of the house. Use some spaghetti for the front path. It's all done!

Fish supper

Here's a chance to make an appetising meal in ten minutes! Enjoy!

You will need:

- Paper plates
- Old magazines
- Scissors
- Glue stick

30 MINUTES

What to do...

From your magazines, cut out patches of texture which remind you of food. Change the menu to suit the food pictures you find.

5 MINUTES

Take a paper plate. We cut these chips from a big desert picture.

The onion is a bit of car, the mushroom is from a forest picture. The tomatoes are – tomatoes!

Add the fish (it's from a jewellery picture) and a slice of lemon (from a fabric brochure).

For a dessert, try the ice cream platter (below, left) or a fruit salad!

Making faces

Collage is perfect for the imagination, you will soon create either a beauty or a monster.

25 MINUTES

5 MINUTES

You will need:

- *Coloured card*
- *Old magazines*
- *Scissors*
- *Glue stick*
- *Tray*
- *Waste-paper basket*

What to do...

Search through your magazines for pictures of faces with eyes, noses, lips, hair, teeth and ears. You will often find them in advertisements. As you cut them out, use a tray to put the cuttings you want to keep separate from waste paper. Cut out plenty of pieces so that you will have a good selection to choose from.

Use coloured card as a background.

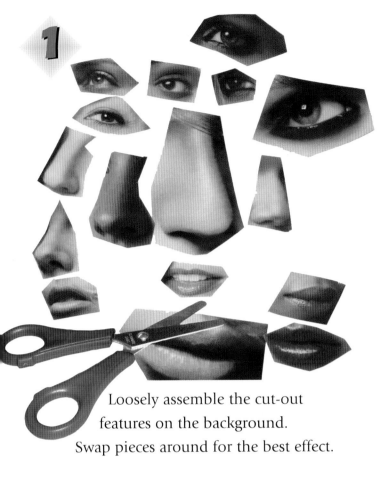

Loosely assemble the cut-out
features on the background.
Swap pieces around for the best effect.

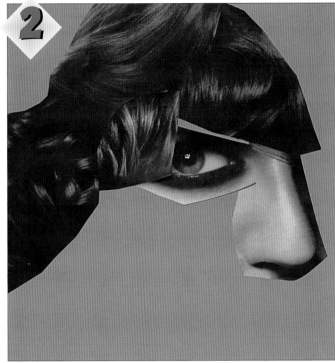

As a face starts to develop, carefully stick down
the shapes. Avoid getting glue on the surface of
the image.

21

Build up the picture with patches of skin colour
and hair textures.

Continue to add to the collage until you are
satisfied with your creation!

Keep my place

Never lose your place in a book again with these easy-to-make bookmarks. Copy the designs opposite, or make up your own.

You will need:

- Thin card, pencil
- Scissors, white craft glue
- Marker pens, crayons
- Coloured paper
- Coloured felt

15 MINUTES

What to do...

Cut out some pieces of plain card, about 150 x 50mm (6 x 2in). Draw an animal head at the top of the card. Paws, hooves or talons should reach about halfway down. Stick felt onto the back of each card before you cut out the shapes.

2 MINUTES

23/05

Broomfield, D

Reserved Item

Branch: Birchington Library
Date: 9/05/2024   Time: 1:42 PM
Name: Broomfield, David J
ID: ...8265

Item: Collage
        c153647938

Expires:23 May 2024

Instruction: Please process item

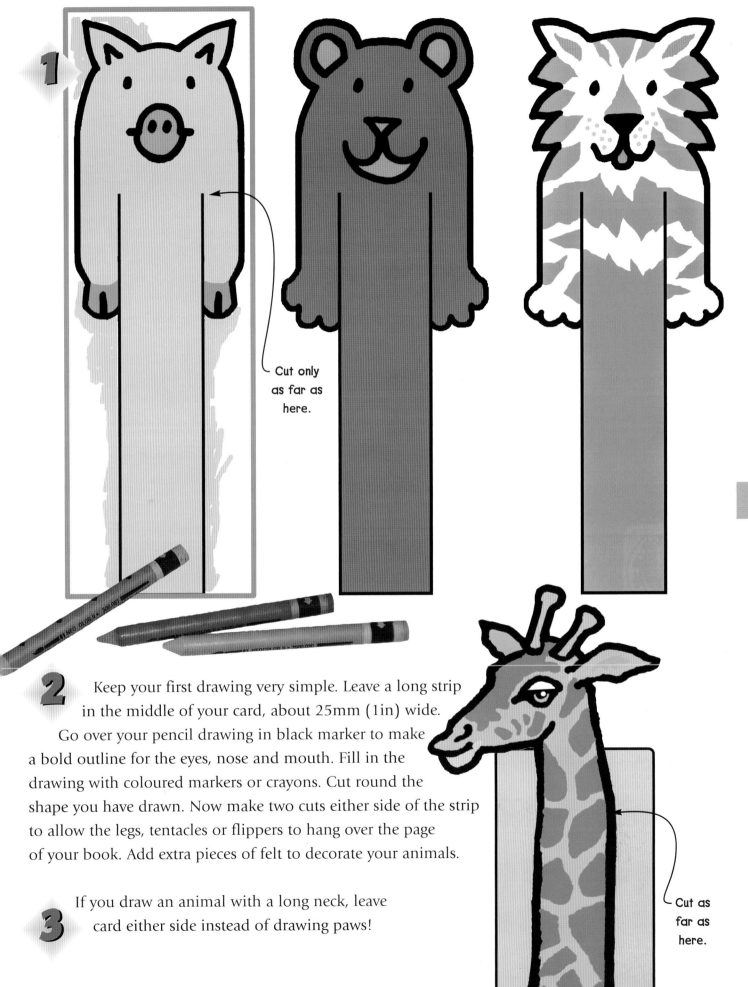

Cut only
as far as
here.

23

2   Keep your first drawing very simple. Leave a long strip
    in the middle of your card, about 25mm (1in) wide.
    Go over your pencil drawing in black marker to make
a bold outline for the eyes, nose and mouth. Fill in the
drawing with coloured markers or crayons. Cut round the
shape you have drawn. Now make two cuts either side of the strip
to allow the legs, tentacles or flippers to hang over the page
of your book. Add extra pieces of felt to decorate your animals.

3   If you draw an animal with a long neck, leave
    card either side instead of drawing paws!

Cut as
far as
here.

Wise owl

40 MINUTES

5 MINUTES

You will need:

- *Coloured papers*
- *Seeds or small leaves*
- *Matchsticks, felt*
- *Scissors, pencil*
- *Universal glue*
- *Marker pens*

What to do...

Choose a brightly coloured sheet of paper for a background. Use cream coloured paper to make the owl's body. Fold it in half lengthways and draw the head, wing and tail shapes on your folded paper. Cut round your drawing then unfold the shape to reveal your owl. Stick the owl's body in the middle of your background.

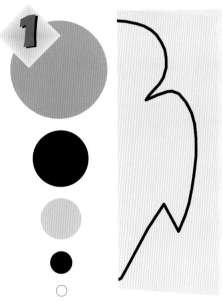

You will need ten circles for eyes. The largest is brown, then black, yellow, black and white. Cut them out from coloured paper or felt.

Stick the eyes on the head of the owl. Add pieces of matchstick round the eyes. Cut a beak shape from some orange paper. Fold it in half lengthways and glue in place.

We have used sycamore seeds for feathers. You could use real feathers or small leaves. Start from the top and outer edges. Stick down each piece, overlapping as you go along.

25

Concentrate on the wings and tail. Leave the cream centre plain except for some little decorative touches.

Add a few feathers to his head. Cut out some claws from coloured paper or felt for his feet. Glue them on.

Allow the glue to dry. Pin the work on the wall. Your first wildlife collage is finished. Well done!

Cut and tear!

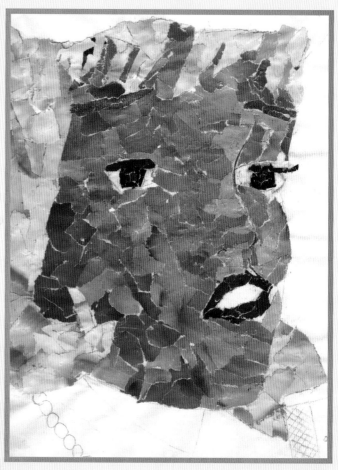

We're cutting pictures from magazines to make faces.
In the collage on the left, we're using things that look like other
things: the bananas look like lips.
In the collage on the right, we're using bits of colour and texture.
We tear the pictures up and use them like a mosaic.

You will need:

- *Drawing paper*
- *Lots of old magazines*
- *Scissors, glue stick*
- *Pencil*
- *Tray*

45
MINUTES

What to do...

Sort through your old
magazines. Make up two
collections of pictures.

5
MINUTES

1

Find a page with a pattern all over it. Cut out a large oval shape.

2

Search for things which look like eyes, nose and ears.

3

Stick down the oval, then add the features! That's fantastic!

1

We made our simple line drawing from a photo of a singer. Use any picture you like, but try a face first. Outline areas of different colours and texture such as eyes, nose, lips, hair and eyebrows.

2

Tear up lots of skin-coloured printed paper from your magazines. The pieces should be roughly 12mm (0.5in) square. Find other colours for eyes, hair and lips. Keep the colours in separate colour groups, like a palette.

3

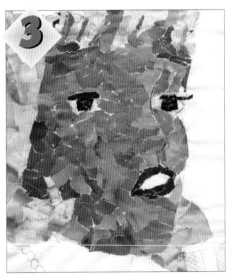

Overlap the pieces as you stick them down. If you need white for eyes or teeth, allow the background paper to show. For small details such as eyebrows or eyelashes, cut shapes from a suitable colour.

Moving zoo

Mobiles are fascinating to watch and quite easy to make. They make a good present for a new baby.

35 MINUTES

5 MINUTES

You will need:

- *Coloured felt, thin card*
- *Coloured pipe cleaners, paper clips*
- *Black thread, sewing needle*
- *Scissors, fabric glue*
- *Tracing paper*

What to do...

You can make your own shapes or use the patterns on page 30. Trace or photocopy the animal shapes onto card.

1

Fix the animal card shape to the two layers of felt with a paper clip. Carefully cut round each animal with scissors.

2

Stick the felt shapes to both sides of the card. Glue on felt stripes or spots as you wish.

3

Use a needle to attach 250mm (10in) of thread to each animal at the place marked with a red dot on the patterns.
Make ten small circles of felt or card for eyes and stick one to each side of the animals.
Use two pipe-cleaners 230mm (9in) long twisted together for the top bar of the mobile. Make a hanging loop at the centre.

4

Use one pipe cleaner to make the lower bar 100mm (4in) long. Hang an animal from each end of the top bar with threads about 130mm (5in) long. Hang three animals from the lower bar. Make the threads 130, 230, 130mm (5, 9, 5in) long so the centre animal hangs lowest. Use a 100mm (4in) piece of thread to fix the lower bar to the top bar. Ask an adult to help you to hang the mobile.

Elephant

Lion

Crocodile

Giraffe

Hippopotamus

Hints and tips

- If you are making different animals, use a pin to find the balancing point shown by the red dot on the patterns above.

Glossary

Cardboard Boxes for packaging are made of cardboard. It's often dull grey or brown.

Corrugated paper A special kind of board made from two layers of paper with a wavy layer of paper glued between them. It's a very strong sort of paper.

Crease A crease is the mark left by folding card or paper and flattening it out again.

Crêpe paper This is a special sort of craft paper made with lots of little wrinkles in it. You can pull it into curved shapes like flower petals.

Diagonal A diagonal is a line that joins the corners of a square or rectangle.

Mobile A mobile is an artwork that can move. They're often made to hang from the ceiling. They can be hung over a baby's cot.

Mosaic A picture or pattern made of small pieces of coloured glass or pottery.

Oblong An oblong is a shape like a square, but longer one way than the other.

Palette This is a tray or board for mixing paints. It can also mean the range of colours that you are using.

Parallel Lines that are the same distance apart (like railway tracks) are parallel.

Pipe-cleaner It used to be used to clean smokers' pipes. Now there are coloured ones for craft work.

Rectangle This is the same as an oblong.

Staple A wire fastener you use to fix paper together.

Template Sometimes called a pattern, a template is a guide for making lots of things the same shape. There are some on the opposite page!

Tissue paper You can buy coloured tissue paper from craft shops. Tissue paper is very thin and is also used for protecting fragile things. Always ask if you can have wrapping paper for your collage!

Tracing paper Thin but strong paper you can see through. Put it on top of something you want to copy and draw on it.

Index